CW00865086

EVERY GOOSE THINKS HIS WIFE IS A DUCK

The Irish Case For Laughing, Crying & Drinking Through Life

By Robert Sullivan

Cover design by William Werber

Graphic Artist: Elvis Torres

ISBN: 1466493135
ISBN-13: 978-1466493131

EVERY GOOSE THINKS HIS WIFE IS A DUCK

To Clare
Cheerfulness is a sign of wisdom

CONTENTS

ACKNOWLEDGMENT

The fact that you hold a real book in your hands (or perhaps, on your e-reader), as opposed to the chaotic pile of quotes and ideas I began this project with two years ago, is entirely due to the help and advice of my wife Susan. I thank her for refusing to allow me to get lazy about any aspect of it, and for helping me see how the voices in it could add up to more than the sum of its parts.

INTRODUCTION

How is it that Ireland, a small fleck in the Atlantic with fewer people in it than Belgium, has created a voice that all the world seems to hear? Lacking armies, it has dispatched legions of high-octane conversationalists who have managed to conquer a part of the global imagination.

Whether it's Blarney, gab, craic or some less tasteful contribution, the Irish always seem to reserve their highest honors for those who can turn the clever phrase. Painters, architects and sculptors seem doomed to comparative obscurity in this culture. Only musicians can hope to, well, play second fiddle. And as important as novelists and playwrights loom in the nation's culture, the spoken word reigns supreme. As a popular saying goes: "In Ireland, a writer is looked upon as a failed conversationalist."

What drives all this eloquent chatter is a quirky world view, once famously called "thinking sideways" by Spike Milligan. It's hard to say exactly where it came from, but my own theory is this: For most of their history, the Irish were governed by foreign powers, often in terrible servitude. They've exacted their revenge by doing what conquerors from the Vikings to the British have never been able to do: The Irish get the joke of it all.

From Jonathan Swift on down through Samuel Beckett (still two of the world's most outrageously modern thinkers), the Irish have developed a knack for looking unflinchingly at all that is absolutely, hopelessly and undeniably ridiculous about life. It's a skill that seems to make people sit up and listen. As a seeker of Irish epigrams, I can attest that among the vast number of printed and online quote anthologies that exist, the Irish seem always to take up an inordinate volume of line space.

This book is not meant to be a compilation of the most important things ever said by or about the Irish. When I began collecting Irish quotes some years ago for a website project, I grew interested in the idea that quotes could form a marvelously compressed narrative of Ireland's story. What's struck me more than anything else in assembling this volume is the consistency of this Irish viewpoint through the ages. It seems as strong and as "out there" whether you look at what they were saying in 1999 or in the fifth century.

Like any country, Ireland is a prism, in which people see different things when they look at it from different angles. I've tried to shed light on a number of those angles by including quotes from the famous, the infamous and the utterly obscure. For good measure, I have included some quotes about the Irish from others around the world who have felt their influence. If I've succeeded, the resulting din will be as fascinating and attractive as the one that's always emanating from that little fleck in the Atlantic.

Robert Sullivan, 2011

A JOKE AS A SERIOUS THING AND A SERIOUS THING AS A JOKE
Irish Philosophy

"That's the Irish people all over - they treat a joke as a serious thing and a serious thing as a joke." - Sean O'Casey, Irish writer and dramatist (1880 - 1964)

"The major sin is the sin of being born." - Samuel Beckett, Irish writer and dramatist (1906 - 1989)

"There's so much absurdity. Poverty is so absurd." - Frank McCourt, Irish teacher and writer (1930 - 2009)

"If suffering brings wisdom, I would wish to be less wise." - William Butler Yeats, Irish poet (1865 - 1939)

"The surest way to fail is not to determine to succeed." - Richard Brinsley Sheridan, Irish-born playwright who owned a theater in London and was a member of the British House of Commons (1751 - 1816)

"Courage is not simply one of the virtues but the form of every virtue at the testing point." - C.S. Lewis, Anglo-Irish writer (1898 - 1963)

"There is always a right and a wrong way, and the wrong way always seems more reasonable."
- George Moore, Irish novelist (1852 - 1933)

"The Irish are the only men who know how to cry for the dirty polluted blood of all the world."
- Norman Mailer, American writer (1923 - 2007)

"There is nothing so absurd or ridiculous that has not at some time been said by some philosopher."
- Oliver Goldsmith, Anglo-Irish writer (1730 - 1774)

"Money couldn't buy friends, but you got a better class of enemy." - Spike Milligan, Anglo-Irish comedian and playwright (1918 - 2002)

"It's not perfect, but to me on balance right now is a lot better than the good old days." - Maeve Binchy, Irish novelist and newspaper writer (b. 1940)

"Humanity, let us say, is like people packed in an automobile which is traveling down a hill without lights at a terrific speed, driven by a small four-year-old child. The signposts along the way are all marked 'Progress.'" - Lord Dunsany, Anglo-Irish writer (1878 - 1957)

"All reformers are bachelors." - George Moore, Irish novelist, playwright and poet (1852 - 1933), in *The Bending of the Bough*

"Who can I tear to pieces, if not my friends? If they were not my friends, I could not do such violence to them." - Francis Bacon, Anglo-Irish painter (1909 - 1992)

"Happiness hates the timid." - Eugene O'Neill, Irish-American playwright (1888 - 1953)

"The innocent and the beautiful have no enemy but time" - William Butler Yeats, Irish poet (1865 - 1939)

"A nation is the same people living in the same place." - James Joyce, Irish writer (1882 - 1941)

"If you look at life one way, there is always cause for alarm." - Elizabeth Bowen, Anglo-Irish writer (1899 - 1973)

"Life is for each man a solitary cell where the walls are mirrors." - Eugene O'Neill, Irish-American playwright (1888 - 1953)

"Life is a long preparation for something that never happens." - William Butler Yeats, Irish poet (1865 - 1939)

"I'm Irish. We think sideways." - Spike Milligan, Anglo-Irish comedian and playwright (1918 - 2002)

"Where there are Irish there's loving and fighting, and when we stop either, it's Ireland no more!" - Rudyard Kipling, English writer (1865 - 1936), in *The Irish Guards*

"Man is in love and loves what vanishes. What more is there to say?" - William Butler Yeats, Irish poet (1865 - 1939)

"The difficulty in life is the choice." - George Moore, Irish novelist (1852 - 1933), in *The Bending of the Bough*

"Every invalid is a physician." - Irish proverb

"May you live to be 100 years, with one extra year to repent." - Irish toast

"Other people have a nationality. The Irish and the Jews have a psychosis." - Brendan Behan, Irish poet and novelist (1923 - 1964)

"All my life I had feared imprisonment, the nun's cell, the hospital bed, the places where one faces the self without distraction, without the crutches of other people." - Edna O'Brien, Irish writer (b. 1930)

"Principally I hate and detest that animal called man, although I heartily love John, Peter, Thomas and so forth." - Jonathan Swift, Irish writer (1667 - 1745)

"The Irish people do not gladly suffer common sense." - Oliver St. John Gogarty, Irish poet, doctor and athlete (1878 - 1957)

"The English are not happy unless they are miserable, the Irish are not at peace unless they are at war, and the Scots are not at home unless they are abroad." - George Orwell, English author and journalist (1903 - 1950)

"Leave the table hungry, leave the bed sleepy, leave the table thirsty." - Old Irish recipe for longevity

"I never wake without finding life a more insignificant thing than it was the day before." - Jonathan Swift, Irish writer (1667 - 1745)

"The devil swallow him sideways." - Old Irish curse

"In order to win you must be prepared to lose sometime. And leave one or two cards showing." - Van Morrison, Northern Irish musician (b. 1945)

"We've never been cool; we're hot. Irish people are Italians who can't dress, Jamaicans who can't dance." - Bono (aka Paul Hewson), lead singer of U2 (b. 1960)

"Ireland is a little Russia in which the longest way round is the shortest way home, and the means more important than the end." - George Augustus Moore, Irish writer, poet and art critic (1852 - 1933)

"The significance of man is that he is insignificant and is aware of it." - Samuel Beckett, Irish writer and dramatist (1906 - 1989), in *Progress and Power*

"We all are born mad. Some remain so." - Samuel Beckett, Irish dramatist (1906 - 1989), in *Waiting for Godot*

"Children begin by loving their parents. After a time they judge them. Rarely, if ever, do they forgive them." - Oscar Wilde, Irish writer and wit (1854 - 1900)

"What do I know of man's destiny? I could tell you more about radishes." - Samuel Beckett, Irish writer and dramatist (1906 - 1989)

"It's my rule never to lose me temper till it would be detrimental to keep it." - Sean O'Casey, Irish playwright (1880 - 1964), in *The Plough and the Stars*

"The typical west of Ireland family consists of father, mother, twelve children and resident Dutch anthropologist." - Flann O'Brien, Irish writer (1911 - 1966)

"I come from an island, Ireland, a nation built upon violence and morose vendettas." - Louis MacNeice, Irish poet and playwright (1907 - 1963)

"I'm troubled, I'm dissatisfied. I'm Irish."
- Marianne Moore, Irish-American poet and wit (1887 - 1972)

"Being Irish, he had an abiding sense of tragedy, which sustained him through temporary periods of joy." - William Butler Yeats, Irish poet (1865 - 1939)

"Money does not make you happy but it quiets the nerves." - Sean O'Casey, Irish writer and dramatist (1880 - 1964)

"Ireland is a fruitful mother of genius, but a barren nurse." - John Boyle O'Reilly, Irish poet and novelist (1844 - 1890)

"Irish Alzheimer's: you forget everything except the grudges." - Judy Collins, Irish-American musician (b. 1939)

"Never ask the children to tell the class what they did for Easter or Christmas or Confirmation or St. Patrick's day...Nothing points up the inequality of people's lives more starkly than asking innocent children how they spent what was meant to be a festival." - Maeve Binchy, Irish novelist and newspaper writer (b. 1940)

"Even when they have nothing, the Irish emit a kind of happiness, a joy." - Fiona Shaw, Irish actress (b. 1958)

"He's a sort of middle-aged man who has very soft eyes but maybe a stubborn look about the mouth; who is happier being silent than talking about his feelings; the kind of man who is happier looking at the horizon than at his possessions. If he was your father," he concludes, "you would know he loved you, but he would never tell you." - Colm Toibin, Irish writer (b. 1955), describing the "Irish Face" in an interview with *The Guardian UK*, April 26, 2009

"The problem with Ireland is that it's a country full of genius, but with absolutely no talent." - Hugh Leonard, Irish dramatist and television writer (1926 - 2009)

"People with a culture of poverty suffer much less from repression than we of the middle class suffer and indeed, if I may make the suggestion with due qualification, they often have a hell of a lot more fun than we have." - Brien Friel, Irish playwright (b. 1929)

"It is a most disgraceful shame the way in which Irishmen are brought up. They are ashamed of their language, institutions, and of everything Irish."
- Douglas Hyde, Irish language scholar and founder of *The Gaelic League* (1860 - 1949), a major Irish cultural organization

"All Corkmen have a hard streak in them. The gentlest are the most cruel. All are cynics. The smilers are the worst." - Daniel O'Connell, Irish political leader (1775 - 1847)

"Nothing is funnier than unhappiness, I grant you that. Yes, yes, it's the most comical thing in the world." - Samuel Beckett, Irish writer and dramatist (1906 - 1989)

"When the wood hardens there is no give in it."
- Irish Proverb

"Resentment is like taking poison and waiting for the other person to die." - Malachy McCourt, American writer (b. 1931)

"There once was a demographic survey done to determine if money was connected to happiness and Ireland was the only place where this did not turn out to be true." - Fiona Shaw, Irish actress (b. 1958)

"Ah, Ireland...That damnable, delightful country, where everything that is right is the opposite of what it ought to be." - Benjamin Disraeli, British politician who held many offices, including Prime Minister (1804 - 1881)

"The true Dubliner is a man who can peel an orange in his pocket." - Niall Toibin, Irish actor & comedian (b. 1929)

"Hard work never killed anybody. But why take a chance?" - Charlie McCarthy, puppet of Edgar Bergen (1903 - 1978)

"Dublin University contains the cream of Ireland: Rich and thick." - Samuel Becket, Irish writer and dramatist (1906 - 1989)

"Here lies the remains of John Hall, grocer. The world is not worth a fig. I have good raisins for saying so." - Legend on a Dublin tombstone

"They know a lot more about Lady Gaga than St Brigid." - George Dillon, in a comment left on *irishcentral.com* about the lack of interest in traditional culture among young Irish people

"The national sport of hurling...the blood and bandages game you called it." - Criostoir O Floinn, Irish writer, in *Sanctuary Island*

"Irish kids are taught mythology as real history. It's different than the way Americans learn about Paul Bunyan." - Tom Kumpf, American photographer (b. 1957) who has photographed ancient monuments in Ireland extensively, in "Ancient Stones & Modern Fears," *The Irish Letter*

"He dug up a fairy-mount against my advice, and had no luck afterwards." - Maria Edgeworth, Anglo-Irish novelist and writer of children's books (1767 - 1849), in *Castle Rackrent*

"The eve of May-day was a trying time, as fairies

were then extra frolicsome in stealing the milk."
- James Bonwick, English-born Australian author
(1817 - 1906), in *Irish Druids and Old Irish Religions*

"Asked if she and her husband believe in fairies, she
replied: 'That's the old folks talking in the old ways,
and neither me nor my Michael believe in any of
that.'
'But if you had a ring fort on your place,' I began,
'and you needed more land to run your cattle, would
you consider getting a bulldozer and dozing it flat?'
'A ring fort! No, not on your life,' she said. 'We'd
never - and thank God we've not got one of those
anywhere near our place - we'd never be the cause
of four generations of bad luck.'" - Conversation
with Irish farmer's wife recounted by Tom Kumpf,
American photographer (b. 1957) in "Ancient
Stones & Modern Fears," *The Irish Letter*

"It is difficult to speculate what may have
happened..." - Spokesperson for the Royal Mail
service, commenting on a postcard that was sent
from Bangor Bay in County Down, Ireland, in
August 1960 and arrived Methven, Scotland, in
January of 2011

"May you live all the days of your life." - Jonathan Swift, Irish writer (1667 - 1745)

A DISORDERLY SET OF PEOPLE
The Early Irish

"...[The Irish are] a disorderly set of people whom no king can govern and no God can please." - Boyle Roche, Irish politician (1743 - 1807)

"The first people of whose existence in Ireland we can be said to know anything are commonly asserted to have been of Turanian origin, and are known as 'Formorians'...a race of utterly savage hunters and fishermen, ignorant of metal, of pottery, possibly even the use of fire." - Emily Lawless in *The Story of Ireland*, published in 1896

"The Irish is a filthy people, wallowing in vice. Of all peoples it is the least instructed in the rudiments of the Faith." - Giraldus Cambrensis (1147 - 1223), in *Topographica Hiberniae*

"It seems to be certain that Ireland continued uninhabited from the Creation to the Deluge." - Abbe McGeoghehan, quoted in *The Story of Ireland* by Emily Lawless, published 1896

"A single legion, with a moderate band of auxiliaries, would be enough to finish the conquest of Ireland." - Gnaeus Julius Agricola (AD 40 - 93)

"Judging from Irish literature...the Druids were, like the Tuatha, nothing better than spiritualistic conjurers, dealer with bad spirits, and always opposing the gospel." - James Bonwick, English-born Australian author (1817 - 1906), in *Irish Druids and Old Irish Religions*

"It is illegal to give someone food in which has been found a dead mouse or weasel." - Ancient Irish law

"There is a perpetual kindness in the Irish cabin – butter milk, potatoes, a stool is offered or a stone is rolled so your honour may sit down and be out of the smoke, and those who beg everywhere seem desirous to exercise free hospitality in their own houses." - Sir Walter Scott, Scottish novelist and playwright (1771 - 1832)

"[Queen Maeve] was imbued, in many stories, with magic powers, including the ability to outrun horses, and to make an army invincible by virtue of her mere presence on the battlefield. Soldiers for the opposition were said to fall to the ground in fits of desire at just the sight of her!" - Richard Cahill, Irish writer, in "Alone With the Ancient Past in Sligo," *The Irish Letter*

"During the first three centuries of the Christian era, chariot-racing was universal in Ireland." - P. W. Joyce, Irish writer (1827 - 1915), in *A Social History of Ancient Ireland*, published 1903

"Ireland is at all points like a young wench that hath a greensickness. She is very fair of visage, and hath a smooth skin of tender grass." - Luke Gerson, in *Ireland Delineated*, published in 1620

"The Irish nobility have in every family a domestic physician who has a tract of land free for his remuneration, and who is appointed, not on account of the amount of learning he brings away in his head from colleges, but because he can cure disorders...Accordingly the Irish are better managed in sickness than the Italians, who have a physician in every village." - Van Helmont, Belgian physician, in *Van Helmont's Confession Authoris*, published 1648

"...as you leave the town, the scene grows worse, and presents you with the utmost penury in the midst of a rich soil. Money is a stranger to them...Their clothes are so ragged, that they publish rather than conceal the wretchedness it was meant to hide." - Edmund Burke, Dublin-born Member of British House of Commons and political theorist (1729 - 1797), describing the poverty in the Irish countryside in 1748

"I have seen the Indian in his forests and the Negro in his irons, and I believed, in pitying their plight, that I saw the lowest ebb of human misery; but I did not then know the degree of poverty to be found in Ireland." - Gustave de Beaumont, French magistrate (1802 - 1866)

"I was deeply moved by the tragic shabbiness of this sinister country." - Henry James, American author (1843 - 1916), after a visit to Dublin

"The legislature have wasted session after session in discussing measures of relief for the wealthier classes; but it can scarcely waste one hour to search for means to remedy the misery in which the mass of the people is steeped. Never was the poor of any nation, either Heathen or Christian, left in so destitute, in so pitiable and forlorn a state as those of Ireland." - Writer of a letter identified as "Justitia" to the editor, *The Farmer's Magazine*, July 1835

"Nothing is so hard for those who abound in riches to conceive how others can be in want." - Jonathan Swift, Irish writer (1667 - 1745)

"In those days duelling pistols were kept at all well-equipped inns. A favourite, but gruesome order to the waiter at night was, 'Call us at six; pistols for two; breakfast for one.'" - Michael MacDonagh, Irish journalist (1862 - 1946), describing the fashion for duelling among "old Irish squires" in the first half of the 19th century, in *Irish Life and Character*, published 1898

"Of all the missionaries that ever preached to the heathen, I suppose St. Patrick was about the most broad-minded and tolerant; as is evidenced in the whole story of his life-work. He made allowance for all the prejudices of the native Irish, and never interfered with any of their customs so long as they did not infringe on the tenets of Christianity." - from the *Shanahus More*, published around the beginning of the 10th century

"William Dycer, the last of his name connected professionally with horses, is no more." - First line of an obituary in *The Irish Times*, May 6, 1861

"The belief about nine waves descended to Christian times. During the prevalence of the terrible yellow plague in Ireland, Colman O'Cluasaige Fereginn, or head professor of St. Finbarr's School in Cork, fled over sea, A.D. 664, with fifty of his pupils, to a certain island, so as to place nine waves between him and the mainland: 'for the learned say' – the old document goes on – 'that pestilence does not make its way farther than nine waves.'" - P.W. Joyce, Irish writer (1827 - 1915), in *A Social History of Ancient Ireland*, published 1903. The yellow plague swept through Ireland twice: in the sixth and seventh centuries.

"We regret to have to state that we have had communications from more than one well-informed correspondent, announcing the appearance of what is called 'cholera' in the potatoes in Ireland, especially in the north." - *The New York Tribune*, October 4, 1845, in one of the first reports of the potato blight that would precipitate the great famine. Between 1845 and 1852, the famine caused the deaths of over 1 million and forced another million to emigrate from Ireland.

"One by one they're falling around us, their pale faces to the sky;
We've no strength left to dig them graves – there let them die."
- Jane Elgee, known as Lady Wilde (no relation to Oscar Wilde), Irish poet (1820 - 1896), in *The Famine Year*

"We do not wish the memory of this calamity to be perpetuated." - From a letter sent by the White Star Line to Father Frank Browne (1880 - 1960), Irish Jesuit priest who rode the *Titanic* from Southampton to Cobh, Ireland (then called Queenstown) and took the best known photos of the doomed ship. White Star's letter was asking Brown to stop doing illustrated lectures on the *Titanic* after the sinking.

"In Sligo we have not been saved from mourning as

four promising young men and women have given up their toll to the ocean. One of the saddest cases is that of our fellow townsman, as we may almost call him, Mr. Alfred Middleton of Ballisodane. Mr. Middleton had a very important position on the *Titanic* and had very probably a brilliant career in front of him. His loss will be deeply regretted by the Sligo people." - *The Sligo Times*, April 20, 1912

"44 Pigs Drowned At Fermoy" - Leadoff headline on a north Cork newspaper on December 8, 1941, the day after Japan attacked Pearl Harbor

"The middle classes think it a sign of vulgarity to speak Irish." - Thomas Davis, Irish writer and founder of Young Ireland literary and political movement (1814 - 1845)

"By the accident of being born in Ireland into families who had lived in Ireland through this past century, everywhere I looked I found people mired in history." - Sebastian Barry, Irish novelist (b. 1955)

"A republic eventually came to pass but the sorrows and troubles never left that tragic, lovely land. For you see, in Ireland there is no future, only the past happening over and over." - Leon Uris, American writer (1924 - 2003), in *Trinity*

HANG THE HARPERS
Musical Notes

"Hang the harpers wherever found and destroy their instruments." - Queen Elizabeth I (1533 - 1603), in a 1603 order to kill musicians who kept traditional Irish culture alive (though the Queen kept an Irish harper in her service to "soothe her nerves")

"I am responsible for two of the worst songs in history. One is 'Do They Know It's Christmas?,' and the other one is 'We Are The World.'" - Bob Geldof, Irish musician (b. 1951), creator of *Band Aid*, which raised over a hundred million Euro for Ethiopian famine relief

"We were looking for new ways of using rock instruments like the guitar, but not in the blues tradition." - The Edge (aka David Howell Evans), lead guitarist of *U2* (b. 1961)

"The first time I saw him [David Bowie] singing 'Starman'…it was like a creature falling from the sky. Americans had put a man on the moon. We had our own British guy from space – with an Irish mother." - Bono (aka Paul Hewson), lead singer of *U2* (b. 1960). Bowie's mother was Margaret "Peggy" Jones (née Burns).

"Wider than the heavens is my fame…I am the best as regards the power of my fingers…Nobody will ever be found to match me." - Turlough O'Carolan, famed Irish harpist and composer (1670 - 1738)

"I live again the days and evenings of my long career. I dream at night of operas and concerts in which I have had my share of success. Now like the old Irish minstrel, I have hung up my harp because my songs are all sung." - John McCormack, Irish tenor (1884 - 1945)

"Pop music should be treated with the disrespect it deserves." - Bob Geldof, Irish musician (b. 1951)

"The Irish are the blacks of Europe. And Dubliners are the blacks of Ireland. And the Northside Dubliners are the blacks of Dublin. So say it once and say it loud, I'm black and I'm proud." - Jimmy Rabbitte, band manager (played by Robert Arkins) in *The Commitments*, 1991

"Rock 'n roll is ridiculous. It's absurd. In the past, *U2* was trying to duck that. Now we're wrapping our arms around it and giving it a great big kiss." - Bono (aka Paul Hewson), Irish singer for *U2* (b. 1960)

"Glorious songs have been in Ireland forever, but a lot of these were so popular they were sung only by drunken men at weddings." - Phil Coulter, Irish musician (b. 1942)

"I never believed it would take off, but, like Martin Luther King Jr., I had a dream. Now Irish music has soared throughout the world. I'm tremendously proud of that." - Paddy Moloney, founding member of Irish traditional group *The Chieftains* (b. 1938)

"You keep sending out these little paper boats, and hope that someday one will come back laden with gold." - Glen Hansard, Irish singer and songwriter for *The Frames* (b. 1970)

"I believe in living. I believe in the old farmer's

principle of letting the field lie fallow. If I'm writing all the time, what am I writing about? Where's life happening?" - Luka Bloom, Irish writer of ballads (b. 1955)

"Being famous was extremely disappointing for me. When I became famous it was a complete drag and it is still a complete drag." - Van Morrison, Northern Irish musician (b. 1945)

"Bring not a bagpipe to a man in trouble."
- Jonathan Swift, Irish writer (1667 - 1745)

"To say what you feel is to dig your own grave."
- Sinéad O'Connor, Irish musician (b. 1966)

"Dancing is a perpendicular expression of a horizontal desire." - George Bernard Shaw, Irish playwright (1856 - 1950)

"If there is music in hell it will be bagpipes." - Joe Tomelty, Irish actor and playwright (1911 - 1995)

"You get lost in the so-called success, people are all around you telling you how great you're doing, how amazing you are – all the while pushing, showing, goading you forward. It got like a monster instead of a beautiful thing." - Dolores O'Riordan, lead singer for *The Cranberries* (b. 1971)

"Of all the interest in world music, the appeal of Celtic music is arguably the strongest." - Pete Heywood, editor of *Living Tradition Magazine*

"After the success of 'Whiskey in the Jar' there was an awful lot of pressure on [*Thin Lizzy*]...People want us to record 'It's a Long, Long Way to Tipperary' rocked up or 'Danny Boy' rocked up...Everybody was coming up and telling us what we should be doing." - Phil Lynott, Irish guitarist and songwriter for *Thin Lizzy* (1949 - 1986)

"Elvis Presley was like God – he was beautiful, he was sexy, he had talent, he had global success. He had anything you could possibly aspire towards – his pick of any woman he wanted. And what does he do? He dies sitting on a toilet." - Paul Brady, Irish musician (b. 1947)

"My advice to you concerning applause is this: enjoy it but never quite believe it." - Samuel Lover, Irish songwriter, novelist and painter (1797 - 1868)

"People assumed I was a lot stronger than I was because I had a big mouth and a shaved head. I acted tough to cover the vulnerability." - Sinéad O'Connor, Irish musician (b. 1966)

EVERY GOOSE THINKS
HIS WIFE IS A DUCK
The Irish Woman

"Every goose thinks his wife is a duck." - Irish proverb, from Mr. *Punch's Irish Humor,* 1910

"I think the Irish woman was freed from slavery by bingo. They can go out now, dressed up, with their handbags and have a drink and play bingo. And they deserve it." - John B. Keane, Irish playwright and novelist (1928 - 2002)

"My only books were women's looks, and folly's all they taught me." - Thomas Moore, Irish poet, songwriter and entertainer (1779 - 1852), in *The Time I've Lost*

"Have you ever been in love, me boys,
Or have you felt the pain?

I'd rather be in jail, I would,
Than be in love again."
- Johnny Patterson, Irish singer, songwriter and
circus entertainer (1840 - 1889)

"The nicest buttocks in the world are in Ireland.
Irish women are always carrying water on their
heads, and always carrying their husbands home
from pubs. Such things are the greatest posture-
builders in the world." - Peter O'Toole, Irish actor
(b. 1932)

"The Irish men are reckoned terrible heart stealers –
but I do not find them very formidable." - Mary
Wollstonecraft, British writer and women's rights
advocate (1759 - 1797)

"A man who understands one woman is qualified to
understand pretty well everything." - John Butler
Yeats, Irish artist, father of W.B. Yeats (1839 - 1922)

"Oscar was not a man of bad character; you could
trust him with a woman anywhere." - William Wilde,
father of Oscar Wilde (1815 - 1876)

"If you want to push something in politics, you're

accused of being aggressive, and that's not supposed to be a good thing for a woman. If you get upset and show it, you're accused of being emotional."
- Mary Harney, Irish politician (b. 1953)

"I think being a woman is like being Irish...everyone says you're important and nice but you take second place all the same." - Iris Murdoch, Anglo-Irish author and philosopher (1919 - 1999)

"Tis only a stepmother would blame you." - Old saying to someone who has committed a minor fault

"I'm simply surrounded by lovers, since Da made a fortune in land. They're coming in clouds like the plovers, to ax me for a hand." - William Percy French, Irish songwriter and entertainer (1854 - 1920)

"I'm not insecure about the fact that I've confirmation-size breasts. It's part of me, and I'd feel very strange with a pair of soccer balls. Having answered that, I insist you ask the lads if they've considered getting their penises enlarged." - Dolores O'Riordan, Irish musician, lead singer for *The Cranberries* (b. 1971)

"There are women in the world who have an ability, not to say a genius, to be given things: houses, jewelry, holidays. And there are other women who seem to be eternally the givers. I don't want to sound totally defeatist, but I would think I am in the second category." - Edna O'Brien, Irish writer (b. 1930), in an interview in *The Atlantic*

"May you die in bed at 95, shot by a jealous spouse."
- Irish toast

"My grandmother made dying her life's work."
- Hugh Leonard, Irish dramatist (1926 - 2009)

"This is a notorious woman in all the coasts of Ireland." - Sir Henry Sidney, Lord Deputy of Ireland, 1576, speaking of Irish "pirate queen" Grace O'Malley

"There was never sex in Ireland before television."
- Oliver J. Flanagan, social conservative politician who served 43 years in Dáil Éireann and was briefly Irish Minister for Defense (1920 - 1987)

"Nowadays nothing is sacred; men marry men, children divorce their parents, a mixed marriage hardly merits a yawn. But fifty years ago the world was a different place, particularly our world, on this small island." - Liz McManus, Irish politician (b. 1947)

"All Ireland is washed by the Gulf Stream, except my wife's family." - Brendan Behan, Irish writer (1923 - 1964)

"Strife is better than loneliness." - Irish saying

"When we want to read about the deeds that are done for love, whither to we turn? To the murder columns." - George Bernard Shaw, Irish playwright (1856 - 1950)

"I value mothers and motherhood enormously. For every inattentive or abusive mother in my fiction I think you'll find a dozen or so who are neither." - William Trevor, Irish writer (b. 1928)

"Once a woman has decided to knit a jersey, nothing short of total paralysis will stop her." - John D. Sheridan, Irish writer, poet and journalist (1903 - 1980)

"I have some women friends but I prefer men. I don't trust women. There is a built-in competition between women." - Edna O'Brien, Irish writer (b. 1930)

"Marry a woman from the mountain, and you marry the mountain." - Irish proverb

"During my childhood, I remember excited, shawled women hurrying to the local public house. On Little Women's Christmas, they would inhabit this man's domain without shame. Sitting in 'the snug,' a small private room inside the front door, they would pool the few shillings they'd saved for the day. Then they would drink stout and dine on thick corned beef sandwiches provided by the publican. For the rest of the year, the only time respectable women would meet for a glass of stout would be during shopping hours, and then only because it was 'good for iron in the blood.'" Sheila Flitton, Irish actress, in "Little Women's Christmas," *The Irish Letter*

"In Ireland, a girl has the choice between perpetual virginity and perpetual pregnancy." - George Moore, Irish novelist (1852 - 1933)

"The most important week in Ireland is the week of the Dublin Horse Show. Grafton Street becomes a garden of girls." - Brian Donn, Irish novelist (1889 - 1928), in *Destiny Bay*

"And Mary, all smiling, was list'ning to me. The moon through the valley her pale rays was shedding When I won the heart of the Rose of Tralee..." - William Pembroke Mulchinock, Irish songwriter (1820 - 1864), in *The Rose of Tralee*

"She's the sort of woman who lives for others – you can always tell the others by their hunted expressions." - C. S. Lewis, Anglo-Irish writer (1898 - 1963)

"She died of a fever
And no one could save her
And that was the end of sweet Molly Malone
But her ghost wheels her barrow
Through streets broad and narrow
Crying cockles and mussels alive, alive o!"
- Attributed to James Yorkston, Scottish musician, in *Molly Malone*, first published in 1883

"Níl aon sean stoca nach bhfaigheann sean bhróg / There's no old stocking that doesn't find an old boot" - Old Irish saying

"Come live in my heart and pay no rent." - Samuel Lover, Irish novelist, songwriter and painter (1797-1868)

CULINARY HINTERLAND
Boiled Potatoes and Other Delicacies

"My culinary hinterland – a place where the traditional approach to food was: if you want to eat something make sure you boil the hell out of it first." - John Kelly, IRA militant (1936 - 2007)

"Luscious [and] heavy, fruit– and fat–laden, and moistened with whipped cream or brandy butter – it's truly heart-stopping stuff." - Regina Sexton, Irish writer, describing Irish Christmas Plum Pudding

"Half a pig and a side of pudding may not sound like an appetizing (or healthy) way to start the day. But that's the 'Full Irish,' and it isn't fading away any time soon." - Breda Heffernan, Irish writer, in "An Ode To Our National Meal, The Full Irish Breakfast," *The Irish Letter*

"Only Irish coffee provides in a single glass all four essential food groups: alcohol, caffeine, sugar, and fat." - Alex Levine

MADNESS SOLD BY THE BOTTLE
The Drinking Life

"A tavern is a place where madness is sold by the bottle." - Jonathan Swift, Irish writer (1667 - 1745)

"That a guest should leave the house sober was considered either a gross breach of hospitality on the part of the host, or a rank offence against what was due to a host on the part of the guest."
- Michael MacDonagh (1862 - 1946), Irish journalist, in *Irish Life and Character*, published 1898

"Virtually every Irish I've known gets mean when he drinks. Particularly the real Irish." - Richard Nixon, American president (1913 - 1994), speaking in February, 1973, on a secret tape released in December of 2010

"In Ireland we drink a lot. It's part of our culture. I

like drinking. I don't think it's a bad thing." - Andrea Corr, Irish musician, *The Corrs* (b. 1974)

"Beer Pong Ireland makes a conscious decision to have the back four cups filled with water, while the other six are filled only slightly with beer. The measures are to ensure compliance with DrinkAware guidelines, and to highlight the sporting – rather than the drinking – aspect of the sport." - Policy of Beer Pong Ireland, the organizer of the Irish Beer Pong Finals, quoted on *irishcentral.com*, November 27, 2010

"The drink and I have been friends for so long, it would be a pity for me to leave without one last kiss." - Alleged last words of Turlough O'Carolan, famous blind harpist, singer and composer (1670 - 1738)

"Drink is the curse of the land. It makes you fight with your neighbor. It makes you shoot at your landlord and it makes you miss him." - Irish saying

"I am, dear Prue, a little in drink, but at all times your faithful husband." - Richard Steele, Irish writer and politician (1672 - 1729), in a letter to his wife

"Be creative in where you take her. Remember...that Americans are not nearly as pub-centric as Irish people and don't need alcohol at every social occasion...Americans often go on dates that are non-alcohol related – which can involve things such as 'cups of coffee.'" - Conn Corrigan, in "An Irishman's Guide to Dating an American Girl," *irishcentral.com*, February, 2011

"There are no advantages to being a tax exile domiciled in Ireland. What you save on tax, you spend on drink." - Spike Milligan, Anglo-Irish comedian and playwright (1918 - 2002)

"St. Patrick – one of the few saints whose feast day presents the opportunity to get determinedly whacked and make a fool of oneself all under the guise of acting Irish." - Charles M. Madigan, American journalist (b. 1949)

"I never heard him cursing; I don't believe he was ever drunk in his life. Sure he's not like a Christian at all." - Sean O'Casey, Irish writer and dramatist (1880 - 1964)

"An Irish queer is a fellow who prefers women to

drink." - Sean O'Faoilain, Irish writer (1900 - 1991)

"Whisky, drink divine! Why should drivellers bore us with praise of wine while we've thee before us?" - Joseph O'Leary, Irish songwriter (1790 - 1850), in *Whisky Drink Divine*

"An elderly man named Sullivan, grocer and spirit dealer, referred a charge against his 'better half' of having committed a series of grievous assaults on him. Mrs. Sullivan [was] a pale-faced, delicate looking woman, commonly known by the sobriquet of 'Featherlegs'...[Mr.] Sullivan having been sworn said that Mrs. S. 'did not leave him a leg to stand on,' he was 'wasting away inch by inch,' and all in consequence of her outrageous conduct. It was not once she had assaulted him, but a thousand times. However, he would do her credit of saying, that she never beat him until she had taken a drop too much, which, however, was, unfortunately, too frequently the case with her." - Article in *The Cork Examiner*, December, 1856

"While it slashed wages and welfare payments left, right and centre (though leaving pensioners, its main support base, largely untouched) the Government –

for the first time in living memory – actually reduced the price of alcohol. This, apparently, is Fianna Fail's master plan for surviving the worst economic crisis in the history of the State - get people to drink more." - Truthsword in "Why Ireland Failed, Part 1" on *HubPages*

"I have made an important discovery. Alcohol, taken in sufficient quantities, produces all the effects of intoxication." - Oscar Wilde, Irish writer and wit (1854 - 1900)

"I loved Jack Ford. I got him in his later days, and he was a total tyrant and a total autocrat and an Irish drunk. But I had a great time." - Richard Widmark, American film actor (1914 - 2008)

"In a country where they found themselves rejected and isolated, Irishmen looked upon the saloon as 'the poor man's club,' a natural transfer of the familiar pub that had always played such an important role in the social life of the Irish countryside." - Thomas O'Connor, American educator, in *The Boston Irish*

"I was a savage for so many years of my life. There

was some seed of determination in me that I was not conscious of. I was mostly consciously getting into trouble and drunk." - Daniel Day-Lewis, Irish actor (b. 1957)

"There has been more written about how I live my life and what state my health is in than about my music. They've turned me into a drunken monster." - Shane McGowan, lead singer of *The Pogues* (b. 1957)

"I love Shane and it makes me angry to see him destroy himself selfishly in front of those who love him." - Sinéad O'Connor, Irish singer (b. 1966), after calling the Police to arrest Shane McGowan and take him to a rehab facility in 2001

"And we were a little bit rowdy when they started toasting the Queen, good Irish boys that we were. And Sean Connery came over and told us to shut up and I told him to f**k off. He backed away and we left, and I can't remember a single thing about the rest of the event. Apparently, I kissed Jessica Lange, but I have no memory of that whatsoever." - Martin MacDonagh, Irish playwright (b. 1970), describing his behavior the night in 1996 when he won the

"Most Promising Playwright" prize at the *London Evening Standard* Theatre Awards

"When Irish eyes are smiling, watch your step."
- Gerald Kersh, English writer (1911 - 1968)

"Normally, when I walk by this building, there are a bunch of people that are totally inebriated hanging out the window. I know that's a stereotype about the Irish, but nevertheless, we Jews around the corner think this." - Michael Bloomberg, Mayor of New York City – in comments about St. Patrick's Day celebrations made in a talk at the Irish Historical Society, February, 2011. The comment drew a firestorm of criticism in NY media outlets, with headlines including "Bloomy's Blarney" and "Irish Stew"

"We all know how sensitive the Irish get when you bring up the fact that their greatest contribution to world culture is Bushmill's Single Malt. They get so angry and upset that the only thing that will calm them down is a nice, stiff drink. Or a drink of any kind, really; they're not picky." - Alex Balk, American journalist, in "Jewish Leprechaun Offends Race of Alcoholics," *theawl.com*, Feb 11, 2011, commenting on Michael Bloomberg's speech at the Irish Historical Society

"I love the plop of whiskey into a glass. I love to see the cream on a pint. I love the first powerful violent impact of a glass of whiskey when it hits the mouth below. I chase it in with a pint and that's even more beautiful still. 'Drink in moderation' is one of the most ridiculous statements ever made. You must drink a little more than moderation." - John B. Keane, Irish playwright and novelist (1928 - 2002), in a video "John B. Keane on Drink," *Youtube*

"A few times John said, 'I'm going to give up drink.' And we said, 'Alright.' And after three days we said, 'For God's sake, go away and take a drink.'" - Mary O'Connor, wife of Irish writer John B. Keane, in a video "John B. Keane on Drink," *Youtube*

"I often sit back and think, 'I wish I'd done that,' and find out later that I already have." - Richard Harris, Irish actor and singer who suffered from alcoholism (1930 - 2002)

"At that beach I learned to swim in the freezing Atlantic Ocean. I had my first go at chasing girls, aged about 11. I was taught my first chords on the guitar. I drank my first Guinness." - Tony Blair, Prime Minister of the United Kingdom from 1997 - 2007 (b. 1953), describing his youth at Rossnowlagh, Ireland

"Let schoolmasters puzzle their brain
with grammar and nonsense and learning
good liquor, I stoutly maintain,
gives genius a better discerning."
- Oliver Goldsmith, Anglo-Irish writer (1730 - 1774), in *She Stoops to Conquer*

THE DEVIL IS BUSY;
YES, VERY BUSY
The Church And Its Influence

"During the intervals the devil is busy; yes, very busy, as sad experience proves, and on the way home in the small hours of the morning, he is busier still." - Pastoral letter from the Bishops, in *The Irish Catholic*, 1933

"Let's just say, I'm Irish. I grew up in the 1950s. Religion had a very tight iron fist." - Liam Neeson, Irish actor (b. 1952)

"Don't be friendly or distant with the Clergy." - Old Irish saying

"An Irish atheist is one who wishes to God he could believe in God." - Sir John Pentland Mahaffy, Irish scholar (1839 - 1919)

"The ultimate role of The Catholic Church in Ireland is the propagation of bingo." - Eamon Keane, Irish actor (1925 - 1990), brother of writer John B. Keane

"'Now which would you rather go to, Father Healy,' said the Protestant, 'to hell or to purgatory?' 'To the latter on account of the climate,' replied the priest, 'but to the former on account of the company - I'm so fond of Protestants.'" - Michael MacDonagh, Irish journalist (1862 - 1946), in *Irish Life and Character*, published 1898

"What they do in heaven we are ignorant of; what they do not do we are told expressly." - Jonathan Swift, Irish writer (1667 - 1745)

"I am between the devil and the Holy See...[My job is to prevent] the Californication of Ireland." - James Montgomery, on being appointed the film censor of Ireland in 1923

"Whenever cannibals are on the brink of starvation, Heaven, in its infinite mercy, sends them a fat missionary." - Oscar Wilde, Irish writer and wit (1854 - 1900)

"A week ago a vast concourse of Catholics assembled at Armagh to dedicate a new Cathedral; and when they started home again the roadways were lined with groups of meek and lowly Protestants who stoned them till the region round about was marked with blood. I thought that only Catholics argued in that way, but it seems to be a mistake." - Mark Twain, American writer (1835 - 1910), proper name Samuel Clemens, in short story *Party Cries in Ireland*

"The notorious fact that St. Patrick lived to be considerably more than a hundred, cut a wisdom tooth at ninety-eight, never had a day's illness in his life...and could see to read without spectacles until within six weeks of his untimely end...speaks libraries for the tonic and salubrious qualities of that stimulating spirit, which has ever since his day been known and highly appreciated under the name of 'L.L.' or 'Long Livers' Whiskey.'" - Charles Keene (1823 - 1891), in *Mr. Punch's Irish Humor*, published 1910

"Honesty is the best policy; but he who is governed by that maxim is not an honest man." - Richard Whately, Archbishop of Dublin (1787 - 1863)

"You've heard, I suppose, long ago, how the snakes, in a manner most antic, he [St. Patrick] marched them to the County Mayo, and trundled them into the Atlantic." - William Maginn, Irish poet and writer (1793 - 1842), in *St. Patrick of Ireland.*

"They would hit you across the face if you got a sum wrong. I suppose they did teach me to read and write and for that I should be grateful, but I'm not." - Colm Toibin, Irish novelist (b. 1955), describing his youth in Irish Catholic schools

"God gives the gifts where He finds the vessel empty enough to receive them." - C.S. Lewis, Anglo-Irish writer (1898 - 1963)

"Aslan symbolizes a Christlike figure...but he also symbolizes for me Muhammad, Buddha and all the great spiritual leaders and prophets over the centuries." - Liam Neeson, Irish actor (b. 1952), on the character he is playing in a film of *The Chronicles of Narnia.* The comment drew criticism from many who see C.S. Lewis, the author of the story, as a hero of conservative Catholicism

"I rebelled against the coercive and stifling religion

into which I was born and bred. It was very frightening, and all pervasive. I'm glad it has gone. But when you remove spirituality, or the quest for it, from people's lives, you remove something very precious." - Edna O'Brien, Irish writer (b. 1930)

"Hearing nun's confessions is like being stoned to death with popcorn." - Fulton J. Sheen, Irish-American Catholic Archbishop known for his television show *The Catholic Hour* (1895 - 1979)

"We have just enough religion to make us hate, but not enough to make us love one another."
- Jonathan Swift, Irish writer (1667 - 1745)

"In some parts of Ireland the sleep which knows no waking is always followed by a wake which knows no sleeping." - Mary Wilson Little, Irish journalist

"Not surprisingly, the combined effects of these sex scandals have driven Irish Catholics away from the church at a time when many were already drifting away...Meanwhile, fewer and fewer young men are entering the priesthood. For people of a certain age, the very idea of an Ireland without Catholic priests is truly beyond imagination." - Patsy McGarry, Irish journalist, in "How Ireland Lost Its Faith," *Foreignpolicy.com*, February 2010

"In no other European nation – with the obvious exception of Vatican City – does the church have this depth of doctrinal involvement in the affairs of state." - Ivana Bacik, Labor Party Senator (b. 1968)

"I think we ought to have as great a regard for religion as we can, so as to keep it out of as many things as possible." - Sean O'Casey, Irish writer and dramatist (1880 - 1964)

"And there's these three girls with the band, I've had lustful thoughts about all of them." - Steve Clifford, pianist (played by Michael Aherne), speaking to priest in a confessional, in *The Commitments*, film from 1991

SCONES FOR THE FUNERAL
This Mortal Coil

"My favorite Irish story is one of a husband lying on his death-bed, moments away from his final gasp. His wife is downstairs in the kitchen baking. He is touched when he smells freshly-baked scones. 'She really loves me,' he thinks to himself. He struggles out of bed and down the stairs, hoping to enjoy a taste. As he reaches to take a scone, she slaps his hand away saying: 'Get your hands off. Those are for the funeral.'" - Clodagh McCoole, Irish writer, in "Death Becomes Her," *The Irish Letter*

"He took me into his surgery...He gave me one of those looks of his, redolent of the cemetery, and said that I should buy day-returns from now on instead of season tickets." - Hugh Leonard, Irish dramatist and television writer (1926 - 2009)

"Death sits easily with the Irish. I think the real reason we love it is that it allows us to 'love our neighbor' without actually suffering them."
- Clodagh McCoole, Irish writer, in "Death Becomes Her," *The Irish Letter*

"Ah well then, I suppose I shall have to die beyond my means." - Oscar Wilde, Irish writer and wit (1854 - 1900)

"One of us must go." - Oscar Wilde, Irish writer (1854 - 1900), commenting on the wallpaper in the room where he was dying

"There's no such thing as bad publicity except your own obituary." - Brendan Behan, Irish poet and novelist (1923 - 1964)

THE GREATEST TALKERS SINCE THE GREEKS
The Irish Tower of Babel

"We Irish will never achieve anything; but we are the greatest talkers since the Greeks." - Oscar Wilde, Irish writer and wit (1854 - 1900)

"Phrases make history here." - John Maffey (1877 - 1969), British Ambassador to London, 1939 - 1949

"The Irish have no sense of destination in their talk." - Walter de la Mare, British poet (1873 - 1956)

"...we filled up the loneliness of our souls with the music of our two voices, dog-racing, betting and offences against chastity being the several objects of our discourse." - Flann O'Brien, Eccentric Irish writer (1911 - 1966)

"Ireland is a lovely country, but very melancholy, except that people never stop talking. Now we're in Dublin and still talking." - Virginia Woolf, British writer (1882 - 1941)

"English is the language of his commerce - the Irish the language of his heart." - Thomas De Vere Coneys, 1842

"The Irish are a fair people. They never speak well of one another." - Samuel Johnson, British poet, essayist and literary critic (1709 - 1784)

"An Irishman can always see both sides of an argument, provided it will lead to a fight."
- J. P. Donleavy, Irish-American writer

"That rare phenomenon, a silent Irishman."
- Winston Churchill, English politician (1874 - 1965), on Arthur Griffith, founder of *Sinn Fein*

"There is no word in Gaelic for goodbye, only for farewell." - Alistair MacLeod, Canadian author and professor (b. 1936)

"Craic is a Gaelic word, with no exact English

translation. The closest you get is 'fun.'" - Elaine Walsh, Irish writer

"Humor is the safety-valve of the nation." - Slogan of satirical publication *The Dublin Opinion*

"My one claim to originality among Irishmen is that I have never made a speech." - George Moore, Irish writer (1852 - 1933)

WOLVES NOT SHEPHERDS
The Blasted British

"I find that I sent wolves not shepherds to govern Ireland, for they have left me nothing but ashes and carcasses to reign over!" - Elizabeth I, Queen of England (1533 - 1603)

"The Englishman has all the qualities of a poker, except its occasional warmth." - Daniel O'Connell, Irish political leader who campaigned for the right of Catholics to sit in the Parliament in Westminster (1775 - 1847)

"To be honest I live among the English and have always found them to be very honest in their business dealings. They are noble, hard-working and anxious to do the right thing. But joy eludes them, they lack the joy that the Irish have." - Fiona Shaw, Irish actress and theatrical director (b. 1958)

"There are three things to be aware of: the hoof of a horse, the horn of a bull and the smile of an Englishman." - Seumas MacManus, Irish writer (1869 - 1960)

"Never remark in England that the air in Ireland is healthy and excellent or they will most certainly tax it." - Jonathan Swift, Irish writer (1667 - 1745)

"All wisdom advises us to keep this [Irish] kingdom as much subordinate and dependent on England as possible; and, holding them from manufacture of wool (which unless otherwise directed, I shall by all means discourage), and then enforcing them to fetch their cloth from England, how can they depart from us without nakedness and beggary?" - Lord Strafford, Lord Lieutenant of Ireland (1593 - 1641), in a letter to King Charles I, 1634

"No person could vote at an election for a member of Parliament without taking an oath that the Catholic religion was false. A Catholic could not hold any office in the civil or military service without taking the same oath." - P.W. Joyce, Irish writer (1827 - 1915), on the Penal Laws of the late 1600's, in *The History of Nations: Ireland*, published 1906

"There is no historical evidence implicating the British government in a conspiracy to exterminate the population of Ireland. But many government officials, as well as those advising them, looked upon the famine as a God-sent solution to the so-called Irish question." - Thomas Gallagher, Irish-American writer (1918 - 1992), in *Paddy's Lament* (Mariner Books, 1987)

"Almost all his loyalties in the colours and enjoyments of life had been burned away, leaving but a slender, intense flame of hatred to what he knew to be England." - Sean O'Casey, Irish playwright (1880 - 1965)

"Now for our Irish wars. We must supplant those rough rug-headed kerns, which like venom where no venom else, but only they have privilege to live." - William Shakespeare, British playwright (1564 - 1616), in *King Richard the Second*

"I never saw him so buoyed up. He said that the first blow had been struck and Ireland would get her freedom, but that she'd have to go through hell first." - Kathleen Clarke, wife of Thomas James Clarke, about meeting her husband before his execution by British forces for his leadership role in the 1916 Easter Uprising

"If England treats her criminals the way she treated me, she doesn't deserve to have any." - Oscar Wilde, Irish writer and wit (1854 - 1900)

"If the devil himself had exercised all his ingenuity to invent a scheme which should destroy the country, he could not have contrived anything more effectual than the principles and practices upon which landed property has been held and managed." - John Bright, British radical politician (1811 - 1889), after being involved in the famine relief effort in Ireland in 1847

"For they're hangin' men an' women for the wearin' o' the green." - From song *The Wearin' O' The Green,* late 18th century

"Negotiating with De Valera is like trying to pick up mercury with a fork." - David Lloyd George, English politician (1863 - 1945), speaking of Eamon De Valera, Ireland's first prime minister. De Valera is said to have replied "Why doesn't he use a spoon?"

"When will it all end? When can a man get down to a book in peace?"- Michael Collins, Irish revolutionary (1890 - 1922), describing his work in the 1916 Easter Uprising against English rule

"I was very nervous about it because I forgot, well I didn't forget, but I was reminded of old paranoias...they all came up when I went to England, feeling Irish, feeling not good enough; all that old stuff I grew up with." - Geraldine Hughes, Irish actress (b. 1970), referring to her performance of a one-woman play she wrote called "Belfast Blues" in 2005)

"Gladstone...spent his declining years trying to guess the answer to the Irish Question; unfortunately whenever he was getting warm, the Irish secretly changed the question." - W. C. Sellar and R. J. Yeatman, English writers, in *1066 and All That*, published in 1930

"The English may batter us to pieces, but they will never succeed in breaking our spirit." - Maude Gonne, Irish Actress and feminist (1865 - 1953)

"Michael Collins rose, looking as though he was

going to shoot someone, preferably himself. In all my life I never saw so much passion and suffering in restraint." - Winston Churchill, British politician (1874 - 1965), on the final stages of negotiating the Anglo-Irish Treaty of 1921

"The English have a miraculous power of turning wine into water." - Oscar Wilde, Irish writer and wit (1854 - 1900)

"…[The English] are the greatest murderers and the proudest people in all of Europe and I am surprised that God tolerates them so long in power – except that He is long-suffering and that His avenging hand is slow but sure." - Anonymous, Quoted in *Elizabethans and the Irish*, by Quinn, published in 1578

"To begin with in Ireland, the most western part of the continent, the natives are peculiarly remarkable for the gaiety and levity of their dispositions; the English, transplanted there, in time lose their serious melancholy air, and become gay and thoughtless." - Oliver Goldsmith, Anglo-Irish writer (1730 - 1774)

"The Irish are the people the English understand least. And we're just not sure...if they will ever really forgive us for the unspeakable sin of not wanting to be like them." - Joseph O'Connor, Irish humorist and novelist (b. 1963), brother of Sinéad O'Connor

"Under the English legal system you are innocent until you are shown to be Irish." - Ted Whitehead, Irish playwright

"Part of being Irish even to this day is not liking the English...Cromwell is like Satan. He drove our family west of the River Shannon to farm rocks 350 years ago! I was raised on that story." - Steven Colbert, American comedian (b. 1964), quoted on PBS special *Faces of America*, February, 2010

"The moment the very name of Ireland is mentioned, the English seem to bid adieu to common feeling, common prudence, and common sense, and to act with the barbarity of tyrants and [with] the fatality of idiots." - Sydney Smith, British clergyman and writer (1771 - 1843)

"Sheep are not considered the most intelligent animals but British scientist say humans may have underestimated the woolly creatures. In fact, the British scientific community is even suggesting that the animals might even be 'Irish-smart.'" - Jon Stewart, American comedian (b. 1962)

"It was a real tough time to be Irish in London. There was a lot of racism. It wasn't quite as bad as it was in the 'no dogs and no Irish apply' era for apartments and stuff like that in the Fifties, but still, the Irish were an underclass in London. I felt very much uncomfortable in London in the early seventies, late sixties. People weren't sure if you were either some mad artistic genius or a terrorist!" - Paul Brady, Irish musician (b. 1947), describing his life in London from 1969 to 1973

"All my best friends are black, gay, Irish or criminals." - Johnny Rotten (aka John Lydon), English musician (b. 1956)

THE DREARY STEEPLES OF FERMANAGH AND TYRONE
Northern Troubles

"Then came the Great War...But as the deluge subsides and the waters fall short, we see the dreary steeples of Fermanagh and Tyrone emerging once again. The integrity of their quarrel is one of the few institutions that has been unaltered in the cataclysm which has swept the world." - Winston Churchill, English politician (1874 - 1964), in a speech at the House of Commons, 1922

"A disease in the family that is never mentioned." - William Trevor, Irish writer (b. 1928), describing the troubles in Northern Ireland

"The gun is not out of Irish politics." - Rev. Ian Paisley, Northern Irish politician and minister (b. 1926)

"My father was an Ulster man
proud Protestant was he.
My mother was a Catholic girl
from County Cork was she.
They were married in two churches
lived happily enough,
Until the day that I was born
and things got rather tough."
- Anthony Murphy, English songwriter, *The Orange
and the Green*

"Abroad, the terms Irishman and Catholic were
synonymous. An Irish Protestant was looked on as a
rare man, a curiosity, a contradiction, a paradox."
- Thomas D'Arcy McGee, Irish nationalist and
Catholic spokesman (1825 - 1868), in *A History of the
Attempts to Establish the Protestant Reformation*

"People don't march as an alternative to jogging.
They do it to assert their supremacy. It's pure
tribalism, the cause of troubles all over the world."
- Gerry Fitt, Northern Irish politician (1926 - 2005),
founding leader of the Social Democratic and
Labour Party

"Anyone who isn't confused in Northern Ireland

doesn't really understand what is going on." - John Hume, politician and Nobel Peace Prize recipient (b. 1937), considered an architect of the Northern Irish Peace Process

"The truth is that Ulster Unionists are not loyal to the crown, but the half-crown." - John Hume, politician and Nobel Peace Prize recipient (b. 1937)

"I can always guarantee that the Irish Citizen Army will fight, but I cannot guarantee that it will be on time." - James Connolly, Irish socialist leader (1868 - 1916), in *Terrible Beauty*

"It's okay once you get the taste of it." - Bernadette Devlin, Catholic politician from Northern Ireland (b. 1947), speaking of being tear-gassed in a 1969 riot in Derry

"Gerry, I can get the army in but it's going to be a devil of a job to get it out." - Jim Callaghan, British Home Secretary (1912 - 2005), responding to call in 1969 by nationalist MP Gerry Fitt to send the British Army into Northern Ireland to control riots

"It's guarded by units of the British army and I can

never come up to this border without experiencing deep feelings of anger and resentment." - Charles Haughey, three-time Prime Minister of Ireland (1925 - 2006)

"The English should give Ireland home rule – and reserve the motion picture rights." - Will Rogers, American humorist (1879-1935)

"I gradually became aware that hailing from the South, or 'Mexico,' as many Northerners call it, could be a liability...My friends from Belfast taught me which pubs and nightclubs I needed to be careful of my accent in. In Belfast, a southern accent might cost you a black eye." - Breda Heffernan, former student from Dublin who attended university in Belfast

"I have made it quite clear that a unified Ireland was one solution that is out. A second solution was a confederation of two states. That is out. A third solution was joint authority. That is out-that is a derogation of sovereignty." - Margaret Thatcher (b. 1925), British Prime Minister from 1979 to 1990

"Buy now while shops last." - Graffiti in Belfast, 1970's

"I was trying to write a play that would get me killed. I had no real fear that I would be, because the paramilitaries never bothered with playwrights anyway, but if they were going to start I wanted to write something that would put me top of the list." - Martin McDonagh, Irish playwright (b. 1970), discussing his anti-I.R.A. play *The Lieutenant*

"Give Ireland Back to the Irish" (song title) - Paul McCartney, English musician (b. 1942). Released shortly after "Bloody Sunday" in 1972, the song was banned in the United Kingdom.

"It's interesting because I go back to Belfast and it's so much better now. And it's like, 'this is great'...there is no fear, and you don't get searched as heavily as you do here (in the U.S.) now, which is quite strange." - Geraldine Hughes, Irish actress (b. 1970), in 2005

MAGNIFICENCE, EASE
AND HEALTH
Crossing Over to America

"We desire, preliminarily, to caution you against entertaining any fantastic idea, such as that magnificence, ease, and health are universally enjoyed in the country..." - "The Irish Emigrant Society," in *Address to the People of Ireland*, published in 1849 as a warning to people in Ireland against believing in tales of easy success in America

"I was called on deck to smell the land – and truly the change was very sensible. It was the breath of youth and hope and love." - Mary Gapper, immigrant, from a series of letters, 1828 - 1842, describing her Atlantic passage from Ireland to North America

"Oh, me little dears dry up your tears

Your parents are too busy makin' money
Oh Mammy dear, we're all mad over here
Livin' in America"
- Larry Kirwan, Irish songwriter (b. 1948) in *Living in America*

"On Sunday last, three thousand emigrants arrived at this port. On Monday there were over two thousand... In four days, twelve thousand persons were landed for the first time upon American shores. A population greater than that of some of the largest and most flourishing villages of this State was thus added to the City of New York within ninety-six hours." - From "Ireland in America," an article describing waves of Irish immigration in *The New York Times*, April 2, 1852

"My Ulster blood is my most priceless heritage."
- James Buchanan, 15th President of the United States (1791 - 1868), whose father emigrated to the U.S. from Ireland

"If this humor be the safety of our race, then it is due largely to the infusion into the American people of the Irish brain." - William Howard Taft, American President (1857 - 1930)

"Though sorry I am to leave the green island,
Whose cause I supported in peace and war,
To live here in bondage I ne'er can be happy,
The green fields of America are sweeter by far."
- *The Green Fields of America*, traditional Irish song

"I wasn't prepared for America, where everybody is glowing with good teeth and good clothes and food." - Frank McCourt, Irish teacher and writer (1930 - 2009)

"At Trinity Law School, the professor asked a student if he knew what the Roe vs. Wade decision was. He sat quietly, pondering this profound question. Finally, after giving it a lot of thought, he sighed and said, 'I believe, sir, this was the decision George Washington made prior to crossing the Delaware.'" - Anecdote sited in several websites

"I have brought up my children to read and write, and there never were children with cleverer heads for their books; but there was no place for them in Ireland, and they have all gone to America but one, and soon he will be gone too." - Peig Sayers, Irish author and seanachaí (traditional story teller) (1873 - 1958), in *The Western Island*

"No man is an Ireland." - Richard Daley, American politician (1902 - 1976), mayor of Chicago for 21 years

"Christopher Columbus, as everyone knows, is honored by posterity because he was the last to discover America." - James Joyce, Irish writer (1882 - 1941)

"In Los Angeles, it's like they jog for two hours a day and then they think they're morally right. That's when you want to choke people, you know?" - Liam Neeson, Irish actor (b. 1952)

"By a kind of instinct, the Irish have attached themselves almost universally to the Democratic party. They got the idea that it was the party of popular rights, the anti-aristocratic party." - Thomas Nichols, in *Forty Years of American Life*, published circa 1860

"One great example of the way (Boss) Tweed really helped the Irish was when the water started to overflow from the Croton Reservoir, it went to certain parts of Manhattan but not to where the poor lived. The mythology of the dirty Irish developed because they had no water, not until Tweed, through aggravation or bribery, got the water to flow through poor neighborhoods." - Pete Hamill, American journalist and novelist (b. 1935), describing Boss Tweed, New York politician of the mid 1800's of Scottish-Irish descent

"Until recently, Irish-Americans, if they made money, disappeared into WASP-dom in Connecticut." - Kevin Whelan, in *The Irish Times*, 1998

"The young men of Ireland who wish to be free and happy should leave it and come here as quickly as possible. There is no place in the world where a man meets so rich a reward for conduct and industry." - John Dunlop, publisher of *The Pennsylvania Packet* (1747 - 1812), born in County Tyrone, emigrated to America at age 10 and fought in Revolutionary War

"I am half black Irish and half old American stock with the usual exaggerated ancestral pretensions. The black Irish half of the family had the money and looked down upon the Maryland side of the family who had...breeding...So being born into that atmosphere of crack, wisecrack and counter crack, I developed a two cylinder inferiority complex." - F. Scott Fitzgerald, American novelist and short story writer (1896 - 1940)

"His gift of gab became known as Fitzblarney, and his followers as 'dearos,' a shortened version of his description of his district as 'the dear old North End.'" - Wikipedia description of Irish-American (Boston) politician John Francis Fitzgerald (1863 - 1950), known as "Honey Fitz," maternal grandfather of President John F. Kennedy

"I spent most of my childhood watching 'TJ Hooker' and 'CHiPS' so I was more familiar with an American accent than an Irish one." - Irish actor Colin Farrell (b. 1976), commenting on his difficulty in mastering an authentic Irish accent for the movie *Ondine* in 2010

"There are still the living to work for, while mourning for the dead." - Rose Fitzgerald Kennedy (1890 - 1995), wife of magnate and political scion Joseph Kennedy and mother of President John F. Kennedy

HE COULD STEAL
A SCENE FROM A DOG
Ireland in the Movies

"He could steal a scene from a dog." - John Ford,
American film director (1894 - 1973), describing
Irish actor Barry Fitzgerald (1888 - 1961)

"It will come to you, this love of the land. There's
no getting away from it if you're Irish." - Gerald
O'Hara, played by Thomas Mitchell (1892 - 1962), in
film *Gone With The Wind* (1939)

"It's interesting, the more successful you become
the more people want to give you stuff for nothing."
- Liam Neeson, Irish actor (b. 1952)

"I'm very proud of my Irish side...I went there when
I broke up with my girlfriend...(but) all you do is
drink Guinness and cry and look at the ocean and

want to kill yourself." - Ben Stiller, American comedian (b. 1965)

"If I make a good movie they say I'm a British director and if I make what they think is a bad one, they say I'm Irish." - Neil Jordan, Irish filmmaker and novelist (b. 1950)

"The weather in Cork is something else. It's the only place in the world you can wake up in the morning and hear the birds coughing." - Hal Roach, American film & TV producer (1892 - 1992)

"I had that stubborn streak, the Irish in me I guess." - Gregory Peck, American film actor (1916 - 2003). Late in his life, Peck was a founding patron of the University College of Dublin's School of Film.

"My first job was a TV shoot and I'm really enjoying the work. I keep my hair in good condition with regular trims and as a dancer I keep in shape at the gym anyway." - Colette Mullarkey of Sligo, who now has a modeling career as a result of the fact that she bears a striking resemblance to Kate Middleton, Duchess of Cambridge.

"Some mornings you wake up and think, gee I look handsome today. Other days I think, what am I doing in the movies? I wanna go back to Ireland and drive a forklift." - Liam Neeson, Irish actor (b. 1952)

"I rather think the cinema will die. Look at the energy being exerted to revive it – yesterday it was color, today three dimensions. I don't give it forty years more. Witness the decline of conversation. Only the Irish have remained incomparable conversationalists, maybe because technical progress has passed them by." - Orson Welles, American film actor and director (1915 - 1985)

VOTE EARLY. VOTE OFTEN.
Political Science

"Vote early. Vote often." - Election saying in Ireland and, later, in Chicago

"Ireland is one of the few countries – perhaps the last - where the boundaries between politics and art have never been fixed." - George Dangerfield, English journalist, literary editor of *Vanity Fair* (1904 - 1986)

"I am careful about my conduct because I know this cause requires clean men." - James Larkin, labor leader known as *Big Jim* (1876 - 1947), who founded the Irish Transport and General Workers Union in 1908

"A land whose countryside would be bright and cozy homesteads, whose fields and villages would be

101

joyous with the sounds of industry, with the romping of sturdy children, the contests of athletic youths, and the laughter of comely maidens."
- Eamon de Valera, Irish politician (1882 - 1975), describing his vision of Ireland in a radio broadcast on St. Patrick's Day, 1943

"Irish diplomacy is the ability to tell a man to go to hell so that he looks forward to making the trip." - Old Irish saying

"He knows nothing; and he thinks he knows everything. That points clearly to a political career." - George Bernard Shaw, Irish dramatist (1856 - 1950)

"Our ancestors believed in magic, prayers, trickery, browbeating and bullying. I think it would be fair to sum that list up as 'Irish politics.'" - Flann O'Brien, Irish writer (1911 - 1966), in *Hair of the Dogma*

"The soldier is proof against an argument but he is not proof against a bullet." - Thomas Francis Meagher, Irish nationalist (1823 -1867) who led a rebellion in Ireland and then fought with the Union army in the American Civil War

"Politics is the chloroform of the Irish people, or rather the hashish." - Oliver St. John, English statesman and judge (1598 - 1673)

"The Dublin Parliament, that noisy side-show, so bizarre in its lineaments and so tragi-comic in its fate." - Daniel Corkery, Irish dramatist (1878 - 1964), in *The Hidden Ireland*

"The majority of the members of the Irish parliament are professional politicians, in the sense that otherwise they would not be given jobs minding mice at crossroads." - Flann O'Brien, Irish writer (1911 - 1966)

"In 1916 militant republicans had another go. Unlike all previous uprisings which were marked by unrealistic optimism, the insurgents this time shrewdly calculated they would lose. They even devised a cunning revolutionary concept known as 'the triumph of failure.' The plan was a huge success when the British not only put down the rebellion but then shot the leaders, thereby alienating public opinion and swinging it behind the rebels. Independence followed for 26 of Ireland's 32 counties." - Frank McNally, "The Xenophobe's

Guide to The Irish." Quote included courtesy of Oval Books: www.xenophobes.com

"Don't learn the rules. Then they can't accuse you of breaking them." - Mary Robinson, President (first female) of Ireland from 1997 - 2002 (b. 1944)

"I'm Barack Obama, from the Moneygall Obamas. And I've come home to find the apostrophe that we lost somewhere along the way." - Barack Obama, President of the United States (b. 1961), on a 2011 visit to Ireland, where his great-great-great grandfather, Fulmouth Kearney, was born

"Whoever makes two ears of corn, or two blades of grass to grow where only one grew before, deserves better of mankind, and does more essential service to his country than the whole race of politicians put together." - Jonathan Swift, Irish writer (1667 - 1745)

"We are not going to apologize for our small role in removing a dictator who made his people suffer for 20 years, carried out horrific acts and didn't care about democracy. He is gone now, and thank God for that." - Bertie Ahern (b. 1951), Taoiseach of

Ireland from 1997 - 2008, speaking in May, 2003 on the war in Iraq and the use of Shannon Airport for US military stopovers

"We were always dead against the war." - Bertie Ahern (b. 1951), Taoiseach of Ireland from 1997 - 2008, speaking of the war in Iraq in December, 2003

"The Irish militia are useless in times of war, and dangerous in times of peace." - George Tyrrell, Irish theologian (1861 - 1909)

"Men have been dying for Ireland since the beginning of time and look at the state of the country." - Frank McCourt, Irish teacher and writer (1930 - 2009)

"Martyrdom is the only way in which a man can become famous without ability." - George Bernard Shaw, Irish playwright (1856 - 1950)

"That's fine in practice, but will it work in theory?" - Garret FitzGerald (1926 - 2011), Taoiseach of Ireland from 1981 to 1982 and from 1982 to 1987, commenting on a suggestion by a political colleague

"In my son's veins flowed the blood of Irish rebels."
- Ernesto Guevara Lynch (1901 - 1987), father of
Cuban revolutionary Che Guevara

"He was a one-off, a unique figure of medieval
power, intrigue and complexity, surrounded by
mystery and money, and protected by populism and
cleverness and the well-timed one-liner." - Maire
Goeghegan-Quinn, former Irish cabinet member (b.
1950), speaking of Charles Haughey, three-time
Prime Minister of Ireland, who died in 2006

"If I saw Mr. Haughey buried at midnight at a crossroads, with a stake driven through his heart -
politically speaking - I should continue to wear a
clove of garlic round my neck, just in case." - Conor
Cruise O'Brien, Irish politician and writer (1917 -
2008), speaking of Charles Haughey, three-time
Prime Minister of Ireland

"Get married again." - Charles Haughey, three-time
Prime Minister of Ireland (1925 - 2006), to women
asking for an increase in the widows' pension

"I believed – and I know this is an unsustainable
belief – in an open door policy. We had to have an

open door policy when Poland joined the EU. We had absolutely no choice. And the Poles arrived in droves. And they added to our society in every possible way. They were good-looking. They were polite. They were hard-working. When you saw them on the street, it lifted my heart. And I felt the same about the Nigerians and the Chinese. And I felt that we had to change our attitudes towards them entirely." - Colm Toibin, Irish writer (b. 1955)

"The more I see of the moneyed classes, the more I understand the guillotine." - George Bernard Shaw, Irish playwright (1856 - 1950)

A STARTLING TRANSFORMATION
The Celtic Tiger's Rise and Fall

"To live in Dublin during the boom was to witness a startling transformation of Irish culture. Once the redheaded stepchild of Europe, we used our new money to dye our hair blond, have our naturally white skin caked with fake tan and our teeth whitened until they glowed blue. Suddenly we preferred frothy cappuccinos to good old Irish tea. We began speaking in faintly American accents, aping the sitcoms we watched on television."
- Donal Lynch, in "The Upside of the Celtic Chimera," *Salon.com*, December 2010

"Ireland is becoming a shabby imitation of a third-rate American state ... We are rapidly losing our identity as a people and because of this, that special quality all Irish writers should have will be lost. A writer is the voice of his people and if the people are no longer individuals I cannot see that the writer will have much currency." - Brian Friel, Irish playwright (b. 1929), quoted by Conor McCarthy in *Modernization: Crisis and Culture in Ireland 1969-1992*, Dublin: Four Courts Press 2000

"There will be no unspoilt countryside left in Ireland just 10 years from now, outside of national parks and mountain peaks." - Frank McDonald, Environment Editor for *The Irish Times* (b. 1950), in "Bungalow Blitz," *The Irish Letter*, published during the building boom of the Celtic Tiger era

"Ireland found riches a good substitute for its traditional culture, but now we may be about to discover what happens when a traditionally poor country returns to poverty without its culture."
- Christopher Caldwell, in "Waiting for Dough, The Luck of the Irish Runs Out," *The Weekly Standard*, May 11, 2009

"Ireland has changed so much from when I grew up – I don't think in a good way. When the common market first came in, you had the supermarkets take over from the basic little old shops. Some people would say it ruined farming, and even ruined all those gardens where people grew vegetables 'out in the back.' That's what happened in the village where my father came from. When the supermarket came, people just drove to it, and stopped growing their own carrots and things." - John Doyle, Irish guitarist (b. 1968)

"This is bigger than AIG...this is bigger than we did with the Bear Stearns. This is a gigantic assignment."- Larry Fink, head of Black Rock Solutions (b. 1952), in January 2011, commenting on his firm's appointment by the Irish government to value the toxic assets of Ireland's six major troubled banks

"Everybody partied." - Irish Finance Minister Brian Lenihan (1959 - 2011), commenting on Ireland's spending spree of the *Celtic Tiger* era

"Lehman's was a world investment bank. They had testicles everywhere." - Bertie Ahern (b. 1951), Taoiseach of Ireland from 1997 - 2008

"Bank of Ireland shares are € 3.80 today. Now if I meet you here next year, or the year after, do you seriously think Bank of Ireland shares will be € 3.80?

I'd go out and buy Bank of Ireland shares...that's what I'd do." - Bertie Ahern (b. 1951), Taoiseach of Ireland from 1997 - 2008, in September of 2008. Six months later, Bank of Ireland shares were trading at 22 cents.

"I tried applying for jobs, internships - even unpaid internships. I couldn't get anything...It's like hitting a brick wall. There's a huge new wave of emigration going on in my country at the moment – it's palpable. I can just see from my own group of friends that I am probably one of the last people to actually emigrate." - Aoife O'Donnell, 27-year-old photographer, telling *CBS Evening News* why she's leaving Dublin for New York, January 2011

"Easily 90% of the sellers in the last year have been Irish." - Phil Cann, English property developer, quoted in *The Irish Times*, January 27, 2011, on the fact that Irish investors who bought up large commercial properties in London during the *Celtic Tiger* era are now bankrupt and desperately trying to sell off the properties

"There really is no good reason for Ireland to have its own banks, which as we can see, haven't been a particular strong suit of a nation that has only taken tentative steps toward reform." - Steve Goldstein, American journalist, on *MarketWatch.com*, 2011

"We've been invaded many times, but never owned." - Michael O'Doibhilin, Irish retiree, commenting on the IMF bailout of Ireland in "Ireland Feels Pain of Crisis In Its Purse And Its Soul," *The New York Times*, December, 2010

"While Irish banks keep their doors open, schools and hospitals will soon close as the country tries to cope with a public-sector deficit one-third the size of its economy." - Jeffrey Rubin, in "Irish and Greek Defaults Will Reshape Europe," *The Huffington Post*, November 30, 2010

"They're all for sale as far as I'm concerned."- Irish Central Bank governor Patrick Honohan, speaking of Ireland's six major banks in "Political Chaos Engulfs Ireland, Threatens Bailout," *Salon.com*, November 2010

"Our history has given us resilience in the face of adversity and maybe it's time to remind ourselves that we do indeed have many strengths to help us on

the journey ahead." - Irish President Mary McAleese
(b. 1951), in Christmas address, December 2010

AN UNCOMMON NUMBER OF LAWYERS
Lawsuit Crazy

"Necessity has no law, but an uncommon number of lawyers." - Irish proverb, from *Mr. Punch's Irish Humor*, 1910

"Laws are like cobwebs, which may catch small flies, but let wasps and hornets break through."
- Jonathan Swift, Irish writer (1667 - 1745)

"The right to pay fees to lawyers is a fundamental and ancient human right, and it is the kernel of what we know as democracy." - Flann O'Brien, Irish writer (1911 - 1966)

"In every half-case, people see compensation. Compensatitis must be the worse disease that we have in the country at the moment." - Bertie Ahern

(b. 1951), Taoiseach (Prime Minister or "Chief") of Ireland from 1997 - 2008, complaining about minor disputes and fender-benders in Ireland generating constant lawsuits, also sometimes referred to as "compo culture"

FOR THE ALLUREMENT OF CONQUERORS
Shades of Green

"Everything about Ireland, her mountains, her streams, her clouds and mist, her dew and sunshine, her music that is the expansion of them all, is made for allurement, especially the allurement of her conquerors." - Katherine Tynan Hinkson, Irish novelist and poet (1861 - 1931)

"No man who has not seen them can imagine the intense desolation of these Donegal moors. Not a man, not a beast, not a cabin was visible." - Dinah Craik, English writer (1826 - 1887)

"The divine harbinger of summer – warm rain." - Kevin Myers, Irish journalist

"Geographically, Ireland is a medium-sized rural

island that is slowly but steadily being consumed by sheep." - Dave Barry, American humorist (b. 1947)

"In a little city like Dublin one meets every person whom one knows within a few days. Around each bend in the road there is a friend, an enemy, a bore striding towards you." - James Stephens, Founding member of the Irish Republican Brotherhood (1882 - 1901)

"Years ago, according to my father, if you wanted to visit the large megalithic passage tomb of Newgrange, you just clambered over some stonewalls and empty fields and walked right in. You reached the burial chamber at the center of the monument by making your way cautiously along a narrow tunnel. Usually, you'd find the chamber deserted, except for the beer cans left by local underage drinkers." - Elaine Walsh, Irish writer, describing how easy it once was to get inside Newgrange. Today there is an annual lottery to choose 50 persons who can watch the winter solstice from within the monument. In 2010, over 23,000 entries were submitted.

"If people want to see the green fields, they should

go to places like Scotland." - Jim Connolly, founder of the Irish Rural Dweller's Association (IRDA) a pro-development group, arguing against any restrictions on development of the Irish countryside, in "Bungalow Blitz," *The Irish Letter*

A POOLROOM
MOVED OUTDOORS
Irish Golf

"A golf course is nothing but a poolroom moved outdoors." - Barry Fitzgerald, Irish actor (1888 - 1961), in film *Going My Way*, 1944

"The people who gave us golf and called it a game are the same people who gave us bagpipes and called it music." - source unknown

"You have a bit of craic and if the golf doesn't go good, well, sure the town's bouncing afterwards anyway." - Ulster semi-pro golfer and writer Johnny Foster, speaking of playing a tournament at Lahinch

"[At Waterville] it's so peaceful you don't even care where the ball is going." - Chad Maulsby, television's *Wandering Golfer*

"Ballybunion is the course on which many golf architects should live and play on before they build golf courses." - Tom Watson, American golf pro (b. 1949)

"If the ball was wrapped in bacon, Lassie couldn't find it." - Irish caddie's comment after a shot into tall rough

"I just dress up what the Good Lord provides."
- Eddie Hackett, legendary Irish golf course architect (1910 - 1996)

"When primitive man beat the ground with sticks, they called it witchcraft. When modern man does the same thing they call it golf." - Michael Neary, Irish golfer

FAILED CONVERSATIONALISTS
Writer's Block

"In Ireland, a writer is looked upon as a failed conversationalist." - Unknown

"An author's first duty is to let down his country." - Brendan Behan, Irish poet and novelist (1923 - 1964)

"Poets should never marry. The world should thank me for not marrying you." - Maude Gonne, Irish actress and feminist (1866 - 1953), speaking of her relationship to Yeats

"A newspaper is a device which is unable to discriminate between a bicycle accident and the collapse of civilization." - George Bernard Shaw, Irish playwright (1856 - 1950)

"I rhyme to see myself, to set the darkness echoing"
- Seamus Heaney, Irish poet (b. 1939), in *Personal Helicon*

"The English language has an unbroken tradition of excellence and when it goes to sleep there is always an Irishman who appears and wakes it." - Carlos Fuentes, Mexican writer (b. 1928)

"Fine words! I wonder where you stole them."
- Jonathan Swift, Irish writer (1667 - 1745)

"One of the problems for a novelist in Ireland is the fact that there are no formal manners. I mean some people have beautiful manners but there's no kind of agreed form of manners." - John McGahern, Irish writer (1934 - 2006)

"Wilde's captors were the police. But his persecutors were to be found on the letters page of the *Daily Telegraph*." - Matthew Parris, British journalist

"Writing is turning life's worst moments into money."- J. P. Donleavy, Irish-American writer (b. 1926)

"Life with the lid on and what happens when the lid comes off..." - Elizabeth Bowen, Anglo-Irish writer (1899 - 1973), describing the theme she liked to focus on in her novels and short stories

"Real vision is the ability to see the invisible."
- Jonathan Swift, Irish writer (1667 - 1745)

"Books! I dunno if I ever told you this, but books are the greatest gift one person can give another."
- Bono (Paul Hewson), lead singer of *U2* (b. 1960)

"Stories, like whiskey, must be allowed to mature in the cask." - Sean O'Faolain, Irish writer (1900 - 1991)

"It was like a miracle; but before our very eyes, and almost in the drawing of a breath, the whole body crumbled into dust and passed from our sight."
- Bram Stoker, Irish writer (1847 - 1912), in *Dracula*

"I have been assured by a very knowing American of my acquaintance in London, that a young healthy child well nursed is at a year old most delicious, nourishing, and wholesome food, whether stewed, roasted, baked, or boiled." - Jonathan Swift, Irish writer (1667 - 1745), in *A Modest Proposal*

"Mr. Yeats...is more concerned with those imaginative traits which have from the beginning been attributed to the Celtic race and which through the Arthurian legends and other medieval sources have modified, it is said, the whole literature of Europe, imaginative traits seen pre-eminently in the mythic idealization of woman and in an elusive sympathy with the energies of nature...The language of Ireland is a refuge from a commercial and imperialistic civilization, he holds, because the people of Ireland still live in a land of dreams."
- Edward Boltwood, in *The Irish Independent*, 1901

"Satire is a sort of glass, wherein beholders do generally discover everybody's face but their own."
- Jonathan Swift, Irish writer (1667 - 1745)

"The play was a great success, but the audience was a disaster." - Oscar Wilde, Irish writer and wit (1854 - 1900)

"A dramatic critic is a man that leaves no turn unstoned." - George Bernard Shaw, Irish playwright (1856 - 1950)

"As writers and readers, as sinners and citizens, our realism and our aesthetic sense make us wary of crediting the positive note." - Seamus Heaney, Northern Irish poet (b. 1939)

"Writing is like getting married. One should never commit oneself until one is amazed at one's luck." - Iris Murdoch, Anglo-Irish writer (1919 - 1999)

"There comes a time when you realize that all stories are more or less the same story." - John McGahern, Irish writer (1934 - 2006)

"It is very difficult to be a hero without an audience, although, in a sense, we are each the hero of a peculiar, half-ruined film called our life." - Sebastian Barry, Irish writer (b. 1955)

"There is an element of autobiography in all fiction in that pain or distress, or pleasure, is based on the author's own. But in my case that is as far as it goes." - William Trevor, Irish writer (b. 1928)

"One by one, they were all becoming shades. Better pass boldly into that other world, in the full glory of some passion, than fade and wither dismally with age." - James Joyce. Irish writer (1882 - 1941), in *Dubliners*

"As our ancestors hide in our DNA, so do their stories. I don't remember saying that, but over the years I've come to believe it. It's as if these hidden people sometimes demand that their stories are told." - Sebastian Barry, Irish writer (b. 1955)

"Years and years ago my grandfather called me to his flat and cursed at me for writing a short novel that was in fact based on the stories I had been told about him when I was a child. I loved him, and we never spoke again." - Sebastian Barry, Irish writer (b. 1955)

"Most of the places are real, and all of the people are made up, but that's not the point. The imagination remains forbidden territory." - Colm Toibin, Irish writer (b. 1955)

"I hear a lot of stories in Ireland, and I read the newspapers. Emile Zola, Gustave Flaubert, the Goncourt brothers – they were always reading the papers, especially the court reports, to find ideas for their work. But you have to pick a story that fits in with your own inner gnaw." - Edna O'Brien, Irish writer (b. 1930), in an the interview in *The Atlantic*, April, 2000

"A writer's journey is a graph. I started with the things I knew – convent girls, family, etc. – but as I became a little more confident I applied myself to venturing into the outer world and, I hope, integrating it with a corresponding inner world."
- Edna O'Brien, Irish writer (b. 1930)

"She changed the nature of Irish fiction; she brought the woman's experience and sex and internal lives of those people on to the page, and she did it with style, and she made those concerns international."
- Andrew O'Hagan, Scottish writer (b. 1968), speaking of Edna O'Brien

"Editors within English publishing houses are always very interested to see an Irish book. Because we sell more. Because Irish people will read the book. You can publish in London, export it to Dublin and they'll buy it. You can publish a book by a young British writer and it could sell none. None. I mean 50. That could never happen with an Irish writer. There would be enough friends, family, supporters. It would be paid attention to in the towns and in the villages. People would think it was important." - Colm Toibin, Irish writer (b. 1955), interviewed by Paul Morton on *www.bookslut.com*, June 2009

"I've put in so many enigmas and puzzles that it will keep the professors busy for centuries arguing over what I meant, and that's the only way of insuring one's immortality." - James Joyce, Irish writer (1882 - 1941)

"Writing a novel is a terrible experience, during which the hair often falls out and the teeth decay." - Flannery O'Connor, Irish-American novelist (1925 - 1964)

"The writer operates at a peculiar crossroads where time and place and eternity somehow meet. His problem is to find that location." - Flannery O'Connor, Irish-American novelist (1925 - 1964)

"My chief desire is to let you see that there is that which is rational, that which is irrational and that which is non-rational – and leave you weltering in the morass thereafter." - Seamus Deane, Northern

Irish critic, poet and novelist (b. 1940), in *Reading in the Dark*

"So the years hang like old clothes, forgotten in the wardrobe of our minds. Did I wear that? Who was I then?" - Brian Moore, Northern Irish novelist (1921 - 1999)

"...mad Ireland hurt you into poetry. Now Ireland has her madness and her weather still. For poetry makes nothing happen." - W.H. Auden, Anglo-American poet (1907 - 1973), in *In Memory of W.B. Yeats*

"I think, perhaps, the best moment, or the best time, is immediately when you have finished something. You have a sense of completion and satisfaction; a job is done. It's just before the period of reassessment when you realize it's not really as good as it ought to be." - Brian Friel, Irish Playwright (b. 1929), quoted in *Brian Friel in Conversation*, by Paul Delaney

"My God what a clumsy olla putrida James Joyce is! Nothing but old fags and cabbage stumps of quotations from the Bible and the rest, stewed in the

juice of deliberate, journalistic dirty-mindedness."
- D.H. Lawrence, British writer (1885 - 1930), in a
letter written in 1928

"To any friend I have left in Ireland after the
publication of this book." - George Birmingham,
Irish judge and politician (b. 1954), in the dedication
of *Up the Rebels!*

"In Ireland they try to make a cat clean by rubbing
its nose in its own filth. James Joyce has tried the
same treatment on the human subject." - George
Bernard Shaw, Irish playwright (1856 - 1950)

"What has Oscar in common with Art? Except that
he dines at our tables and picks from our platters the
plums for the puddings he peddles in the provinces.
Oscar - the amiable, irresponsible, esruent Oscar -
with no more sense of a picture than of the fit of a
coat, as the courage of the opinions – of others!"
- James McNeill Whistler, American painter (1834 -
1903), in a letter written during a lengthy public feud
with Oscar Wilde in 1886

"A literary movement is five or six people who live
in the same town and hate each other." - George

Russell, Irish writer, editor and nationalist (1867 - 1935)

"James Joyce was a synthesizer, trying to bring in as much as he could. I am an analyzer, trying to leave out as much as I can." - Samuel Beckett, Irish writer and dramatist (1906 - 1989)

"There is a tendency among the young playwrights today to feel that the interpretations that playwrights have been using are not the truth and that the only way to get at people is through showing them events. But this is not the function of the theater." - Brian Friel, Irish Playwright (b. 1929), quoted in *Brian Friel in Conversation*, by Paul Delaney

"When I was ten I read fairy tales in secret. Now that I am 50 I read them openly. When I became a man I put away childish things, including the fear of childishness." - C.S. Lewis, Anglo-Irish writer (1898 - 1963)

"The past appeared to me in the light of a frightful dream; yet the vessel in which I was, the wind that blew me from the detested shore of Ireland, and the sea which surrounded me told me too forcibly that I was deceived by no vision and that Clerval, my friend and dearest companion, had fallen a victim to me and the monster of my creation." - Mary Shelley, English writer (1797 - 1851), in *Frankenstein*

"The most famous building in the heart of Dublin is the architecturally undistinguished Abbey Theatre, once the city morgue and now entirely restored to its original purpose." - Frank O'Connor, Irish writer (1903 - 1966)

"All artists are vain, they long to be recognized and to leave something to posterity. They want to be loved, and at the same time they want to be free. But nobody is free." - Francis Bacon, Anglo-Irish painter (1909 - 1992)

"All art is quite useless." - Oscar Wilde, Irish writer and wit (1854 - 1900)

"Poets are sultans, if they had their will; for every author would his brother kill." - Roger Boyle, Irish playwright and soldier (1621 - 1679)

"Oscar Wilde paraphrased and inverted the witticisms and epigrams of others. His method of literary piracy was on the lines of the robber Cacus, who dragged stolen cows backwards by the tails to his cavern so that their hoof-prints might not lead to detection." - George Moore, Irish novelist (1852 - 1933)

"Reading made Don Quixote a gentleman. Believing what he read made him mad." - George Bernard Shaw, Irish playwright (1856 - 1950)

"The best way to make your audience laugh is to start laughing yourself." - Oliver Goldsmith, Anglo-Irish writer (1730 - 1774)

ABOUT THE AUTHOR

Robert Sullivan grew up in an Irish-German household in the New York City area. His relationship with his maternal grandfather, who was born in County Kerry, formed the foundation for a long-running interest in Ireland and Irish culture. It grew on a first visit to Ireland in 1975. Staying in the simple cottage of his grandfather's step-sister in a remote outpost on the Beara Peninsula, he became fascinated with the durability of Irish culture, even in the face of the country's rapid modernization. After several return visits, he created a newsletter for Irish-Americans called The Irish Letter (no longer published) and a website ireland-fun-facts.com, which have allowed him to indulge his ongoing fascination with all that makes Ireland unique. This is his second book. His first is "The Great Little Book of Fun Things You Probably Don't Know About Ireland."

2068719R00074

Printed in Great Britain
by Amazon.co.uk, Ltd.,
Marston Gate.